G000166859

CAMBRIDGE POETS

OLEANDER PRESS

The Oleander Press
16 Orchard Street
Cambridge
CB1 1JT
www.oleanderpress.com

Introduction © Dan Healy

ISBN: 9781909349261

Designed and typeset by Ayshea Carter
manganese@ntlworld.com
Cover image: The Bridge of Sighs (By kind permission of the Master
and Fellows of St John's College, Cambridge)

Printed in England

CAMBRIDGE POETS

Edited by

DAN HEALY

OLEANDER PRESS

CONTENTS

INTRODUCTION

This anthology of Cambridge poets has been compiled for a very simple reason, that is, there wasn't one. It is not meant to be a scholarly appreciation. Rather, it is designed as a diverting introduction. For this reason it is an eclectic mixture of the great, the good, and the barely remembered. All of whom, at one time or another, have studied at Cambridge. Many of them did not complete their degrees, this was a common practice in the earlier years of the University and was not necessarily seen as a failure. Rather, it was an accumulation of knowledge, of friends and, of course, of fun.

The biographical introductions to the poets are pithy, designed to interest the many who have little or no knowledge of them. Small hooks that, I hope, will lead you into a further reading of these poets' works, with the possible exception of Thomas Shadwell. If, like myself, you were taught poetry at school – you have my commiserations. I hope that this volume may go some way to redressing that balance.

Finally, there are a couple of terms which require an explanation.

1. Sizar: those that, in return for room and board, performed chores at the University.

2. The Cambridge Apostles: a secret society founded in

1820 devoted to intellectual pursuits (probably). Known as apostles because there are only twelve members at any one time. Although a 'secret society', I doubt there are any sinister overtones for the conspiracy-minded theorists among you. For that, you have my apologies. However, Anthony Blunt and Guy Burgess were once members if that is any help.

Dan Healy

Harvey, Gabriel (1545-1630)

Christ's College

Born in Saffron Walden, the son of a rope maker. After matriculating at Christ's he was elected a Fellow of Pembroke. Although a great friend of Edmund Spenser it seems he was not well liked by anyone else. Indeed, feeling against him was so strong in his own college that the fellows delayed 3 months before allowing him the necessary grace for his MA. For that, if for no other reason, I've included him here.

He was famously embroiled in an argument with Thomas Nashe who wrote of him, "he goes twitching and hopping in our language like a man running upon quagmires, up the hill in one syllable, and down the dale in another".

Speculum Tuscanismi

Since Galatea came in, and Tuscanism gan usurp,
Vanity above all: villainy next her, stateliness Empress
No man but minion, stout, lout, plain, swain, quoth a Lording:
No words but valorous, no works but womanish only.
For life Magnificoes, not a beck but glorious in show,
In deed most frivolous, not a look but Tuscanish always.
His cringing side neck, eyes glancing, fisnamy smirking,
With forefinger kiss, and brave embrace to the footward.

Large bellied Cod-pieced doublet, uncod-pieced half hose,
Straight to the dock like a shirt, and close to the britch like a
diveling.
A little Apish flat couched fast to the pate like an oyster,
French camarick ruffs, deep with a whiteness starched to the
purpose.
Every one A per se A, his terms and braveries in print,
Delicate in speech, quaint in array: conceited in all points,
In Courtly guiles a passing singular odd man,
For Gallants a brave Mirror, a Primrose of Honour,
A Diamond for nonce, a fellow peerless in England.
Not the like discourser for Tongue, and head to be found out,
Not the like resolute man for great and serious affairs,
Not the like Lynx to spy out secrets and privities of States,
Eyed like to Argus, eared like to Midas, nos'd like to Naso,
Wing'd like to Mercury, fittst of a thousand for to be employ'd,
This, nay more than this, doth practice of Italy in one year.
None do I name, but some do I know, that a piece of a twelve
month
Hath so perfited outly and inly both body, both soul,
That none for sense and senses half matchable with them.
A vulture's smelling, Ape's tasting, sight of an eagle,
A spider's touching, Hart's hearing, might of a Lion.
Compounds of wisdom, wit, prowess, bounty, behavior,
All gallant virtues, all qualities of body and soul.
O thrice ten hundred thousand times blessed and happy,
Blessed and happy travail, Travailer most blessed and happy.
"Tell me in good sooth, doth it not too evidently appear
that this English poet wanted but a good pattern before his
eyes,
as it might be some delicate and choice elegant Poesy
of good Master Sidney's or Master Dyer's
(our very Castor and Pollux for such and many greater
matters)
when this trim gear was in the matching?"

Spenser, Edmund (1552-1599)

Pembroke College

Spenser received both a BA and MA. It is probable that he was a sizar, a student with limited means who in return for room and board performed chores around the college. In the *Faerie Queene* (IV.xi.34) Spenser refers to the University as "my mother Cambridge".

'Joy of my life, full oft for loving you'

Joy of my life, full oft for loving you
I bless my lot, that was so lucky placed:
But then the more your own mishap I rue,
That are so much by so mean love embased.
For had the equal heavens so much you graced
In this as in the rest, ye might invent
Some heavenly wit, whose verse could have enchased
Your glorious name in golden monument.
But since ye deign'd so goodly to relent
To me your thrall, in whom is little worth,
That little that I am shall all be spent
In setting your immortal praises forth;
Whose lofty argument uplifting me
Shall lift you up unto an high degree.

Prosopopoia: or Mother Hubbard's Tale

By that he ended had his ghostly sermon,
The fox was well induc'd to be a parson,
And of the priest eftsoons gan to inquire,
How to a benefice he might aspire.
"Marry, there" (said the priest) "is art indeed:
Much good deep learning one thereout may read;
For that the ground-work is, and end of all,
How to obtain a beneficial.
First, therefore, when ye have in handsome wise
Yourself attired, as you can devise,
Then to some nobleman yourself apply,
Or other great one in the worldes eye,
That hath a zealous disposition
To God, and so to his religion.
There must thou fashion eke a godly zeal,
Such as no carpers may contrare reveal;
For each thing feigned ought more wary be.
There thou must walk in sober gravity,
And seem as saint-like as Saint Radegund:
Fast much, pray oft, look lowly on the ground,
And unto every one do courtesy meek:
These looks (nought saying) do a benefice seek,
But be thou sure one not to lack or long.
And if thee list unto the court to throng,
And there to hunt after the hoped prey,
Then must thou thee dispose another way:
For there thou needs must learn to laugh, to lie,
To face, to forge, to scoff, to company,
To crouch, to please, to be a beetle-stock
Of thy great master's will, to scorn, or mock.
So may'st thou chance mock out a benefice,
Unless thou canst one conjure by device,
Or cast a figure for a bishopric;

And if one could, it were but a school trick.
These be the ways by which without reward
Livings in court be gotten, though full hard;
For nothing there is done without a fee:
The courtier needs must recompensed be
With a benevolence, or have in gage
The primitias of your parsonage:
Scarce can a bishopric forpass them by,
But that it must be gelt in privity.
Do not thou therefore seek a living there,
But of more private persons seek elsewhere,
Whereas thou may'st compound a better penny,
Ne let thy learning question'd be of any.
For some good gentleman, that hath the right
Unto his church for to present a wight,
Will cope with thee in reasonable wise;
That if the living yearly do arise
To forty pound, that then his youngest son
Shall twenty have, and twenty thou hast won:
Thou hast it won, for it is of frank gift,
And he will care for all the rest to shift,
Both that the bishop may admit of thee,
And that therein thou may'st maintained be.
This is the way for one that is unlearn'd
Living to get, and not to be discern'd.
But they that are great clerks, have nearer ways,
For learning sake to living them to raise;
Yet many eke of them (God wot) are driven
T' accept a benefice in pieces riven.
How say'st thou (friend), have I not well discourst
Upon this common-place (though plain, not worst)?
Better a short tale than a bad long shriving.
Needs any more to learn to get a living?"

"Now sure, and by my halidom," (quoth he)
"Ye a great master are in your degree:
Great thanks I yield you for your discipline,
And do not doubt but duly to incline
My wits thereto, as ye shall shortly hear."
The priest him wish'd good speed, and well to fare:
So parted they, as either's way them led.
But th' ape and fox ere long so well them sped,
Through the priest's wholesome counsel lately taught,
And through their own fair handling wisely wrought,
That they a benefice 'twixt them obtained;
And crafty Reynold was a priest ordained,
And th' ape his parish clerk procur'd to be.
Then made they revel rout and goodly glee;
But, ere long time had passed, they so ill
Did order their affairs, that th' evil will
Of all their parish'ners they had constrain'd;
Who to the Ordinary of them complain'd,
How foully they their offices abus'd,
And them of crimes and heresies accus'd,
That pursuivants he often for them sent;
But they neglected his commandement.
So long persisted obstinate and bold,
Till at the length he published to hold
A visitation, and them cited thether:
Then was high time their wits about to geather.
What did they then, but made a composition
With their next neighbour priest, for light condition,
To whom their living they resigned quite
For a few pence, and ran away by night.

Iambicum Trimetrum

Unhappy verse, the witness of my unhappy state,
    Make thy self flutt'ring wings of thy fast flying
      Thought, and fly forth unto my love, wheresoever she be:
Whether lying restless in heavy bed, or else
    Sitting so cheerless at the cheerful board, or else
      Playing alone careless on her heavenly virginals.
If in bed, tell her, that my eyes can take no rest:
    If at board, tell her, that my mouth can eat no meat:
      If at her virginals, tell her, I can hear no mirth.
Asked why? say: waking love suffereth no sleep:
    Say that raging love doth appal the weak stomach:
      Say, that lamenting love marreth the musical.
Tell her, that her pleasures were wont to lull me asleep:
    Tell her, that her beauty was wont to feed mine eyes:
      Tell her, that her sweet tongue was wont to make me mirth.
Now do I nightly waste, wanting my kindly rest:
    Now do I daily starve, wanting my lively food:
      Now do I always die, wanting thy timely mirth.
And if I waste, who will bewail my heavy chance?
    And if I starve, who will record my cursed end?
      And if I die, who will say: "This was Immerito"?

Nashe, Thomas (1567-1601)

St John's College

Nashe was a sizar at St John's before obtaining his degree. He was probably unable to continue his MA because of a lack of funds following the death of his father. He was one of the greatest prose stylists of his day. One who never shirked an argument, instead he seemed to positively revel in them, famously with Gabriel Harvey.

Spring, the sweet spring

Spring, the sweet spring, is the year's pleasant king,
Then blooms each thing, then maids dance in a ring,
Cold doth not sting, the pretty birds do sing:
Cuckoo, jug-jug, pu-we, to-witta-woo!

The palm and may make country houses gay,
Lambs frisk and play, the shepherds pipe all day,
And we hear aye birds tune this merry lay:
Cuckoo, jug-jug, pu-we, to-witta-woo!

The fields breathe sweet, the daisies kiss our feet,
Young lovers meet, old wives a-sunning sit,
In every street these tunes our ears do greet:
Cuckoo, jug-jug, pu-we, to witta-woo!

Adieu, Farewell, Earth's Bliss

Adieu, farewell earth's bliss,
This world uncertain is:
Fond are life's lustful joys,
Death proves them all but toys.
None from his darts can fly:
I am sick, I must die.
Lord have mercy on us!

Rich men, trust not in wealth,
Gold cannot buy you health;
Physic himself must fade,
All things to end are made;
The plague full swift goes by:
I am sick, I must die.
Lord have mercy on us!

Beauty is but a flower,
Which wrinkles will devour;
Brightness falls from the air,
Queens have died young and fair,
Dust hath closèd Helen's eye:
I am sick, I must die.
Lord have mercy on us!

Strength stoops unto the grave,
Worms feed on Hector brave,
Swords may not fight with fate,
Earth still holds ope her gate.
Come, come, the bells do cry,
I am sick, I must die.
Lord have mercy on us!

Haste therefore each degree
To welcome destiny;
Heaven is our heritage
Earth but a player's stage,
Mount we unto the sky:
I am sick, I must die.
Lord have mercy on us!

Fletcher, John (1579-1625)

Corpus Christi College

Believed to have entered Corpus Christi (then known as Benet college) at the tender age of eleven. Known primarily as a dramatist, it is believed that he collaborated with Shakespeare and succeeded him as playwright for the King's Men. He also wrote a sequel to the *Taming of the Shrew* called 'The Woman's Prize'. He died of the plague.

Take, Oh, Take Those Lips Away

Take, oh, take those lips away
That so sweetly were forsworn
And those eyes, like break of day,
Lights that do mislead the morn;
But my kisses bring again,
Seals of love, though sealed in vain.

Hide, oh, hide those hills of snow,
Which thy frozen bosom bears,
On whose tops the pinks that grow
Are of those that April wears;
But first set my poor heart free,
Bound in those icy chains by thee.

Beauty Clear and Fair

Beauty clear and fair,
　　Where the air
Rather like a perfume dwells;
　　Where the violet and the rose
　　Their blue veins and blush disclose,
And come to honour nothing else:
　　Where to live near
　　And planted there
Is to live, and still live new;
　　Where to gain a favour is
　　More than light, perpetual bliss--
Make me live by serving you!

Dear, again back recall
　　To this light,
A stranger to himself and all!
　　Both the wonder and the story
　　Shall be yours, and eke the glory;
I am your servant, and your thrall.

Hence, All You Vain Delights from the Nice Valour

Hence, all you vain delights,
As short as are the nights
Wherein you spend your folly:
There's nought in this life sweet,
If man were wise to see't,
But only melancholy,
O sweetest melancholy!
Welcome, folded arms, and fixed eyes,
A sigh that piercing mortifies,
A look that's fastened to the ground,

A tongue chained up without a sound;
Fountain-heads, and pathless groves,
Places which pale passion loves;
Moonlight walks, when all the fowls
Are warmly housed, save bats and owls;
A midnight bell, a parting groan:
These are the sounds we feed upon;
Then stretch our bones in a still gloomy valley,
Nothing's so dainty sweet as lovely melancholy.

The Power of Music

ORPHEUS with his lute made trees,
And the mountain-tops that freeze,
Bow themselves when he did sing:
To his music plants and flowers
Ever sprung; as sun and showers
There had made a lasting spring.

Everything that heard him play,
Even the billows of the sea,
Hung their heads, and then lay by.

In sweet music is such art,
Killing care and grief of heart
Fall asleep, or, hearing, die.

Herbert, George (1593-1633)

Trinity College

Born in Wales. A metaphysical poet and priest. A slightly different figure from other Cambridge poets in having a successful academic career; not only did he obtain a degree, he also went on to get a Masters at the age of twenty. Elected a major fellow and reader in rhetoric, he was also the Cambridge University orator. Some of his poems have become hymns.

Sweet

Sweet day, so cool, so calm, so bright!
The bridal of the earth and sky –
The dew shall weep thy fall to-night;
For thou must die.

Sweet rose, whose hue angry and brave
Bids the rash gazer wipe his eye,
Thy root is ever in its grave,
And thou must die.

Sweet spring, full of sweet days and roses,
A box where sweets compacted lie,
My music shows ye have your closes,
And all must die.

Only a sweet and virtuous soul,
Like season'd timber, never gives;
But though the whole world turn to coal,
Then chiefly lives.

The Quip

The merry World did on a day
With his train-bands and mates agree
To meet together where I lay,
And all in sport to jeer at me.

First Beauty crept into a rose,
Which when I pluck'd not, "Sir," said she,
"Tell me, I pray, whose hands are those?"
But Thou shalt answer, Lord, for me.

Then Money came, and chinking still,
"What tune is this, poor man?" said he;
"I heard in music you had skill:"
But Thou shalt answer, Lord, for me.

Then came brave Glory puffing by
In silks that whistled, who but he?
He scarce allow'd me half an eye:
But Thou shalt answer, Lord, for me.

Then came quick Wit and Conversation,
And he would needs a comfort be,
And, to be short, make an oration:
But Thou shalt answer, Lord, for me.

Yet when the hour of Thy design
To answer these fine things shall come,
Speak not at large, say, I am Thine;
And then they have their answer home.

Vanity

The fleet astronomer can bore
And thread the spheres with his quick-piercing mind:
He views their stations, walks from door to door,
    Surveys, as if he had designed
To make a purchase there; he sees their dances,
        And knoweth long before
Both their full-eyes aspècts, and secret glances.

    The nimble diver with his side
Cuts through the working waves, that he may fetch
His dearly-earnèd pearl, which God did hide
    On purpose from the venturous wretch;
That he might save his life, and also hers
        Who with excessive pride
Her own destruction and his danger wears.

    The subtle chymic can divest
And strip the creature naked, till he find
The callow principles within their nest:
    There he imparts to them his mind,
Admitted to their bed-chamber, before
        They appear trim and dressed
To ordinary suitors at the door.

    What hath not man sought out and found,
But his dear God? who yet his glorious law
Embosoms in us, mellowing the ground

With showers and frosts, with love and awe,
So that we need not say, "Where's this command?"
                    Poor man, thou searchest round
To find out death, but missest life at hand.

Milton, John   (1608-1674)

Christ's College

Although a good student, in 1626 Milton was rusticated (suspended) following a disagreement with one of his tutors. After this he obtained both a BA and MA. Because of his long hair and feminine appearance he was known as the Lady of Christ's.

One of the greatest English poets. Milton was a supporter of Cromwell, falling out of favour somewhat after the Restoration by which time he was completely blind. Partly due to his reputation and partly due to my inability to find anything shorter I've included one of his longer poems. He apparently died of complications arising from gout.

To Mr. Lawrence

Lawrence, of virtuous father virtuous son,
    Now that the fields are dank, and ways are mire,
    Where shall we sometimes meet, and by the fire
    Help waste a sullen day; what may be won
From the hard season gaining? Time will run
    On smoother, till Favonius re-inspire
    The frozen earth, and clothe in fresh attire
    The lily and rose, that neither sow'd nor spun.

What neat repast shall feast us, light and choice,
    Of Attic taste, with wine, whence we may rise
    To hear the lute well touch'd, or artful voice
Warble immortal notes and Tuscan air?
    He who of those delights can judge, and spare
    To interpose them oft, is not unwise.

Sonnet XVI: To the Lord General Cromwell

Cromwell, our chief of men, who through a cloud
    Not of war only, but detractions rude,
    Guided by faith and matchless fortitude,
    To peace and truth thy glorious way hast plough'd,
And on the neck of crowned Fortune proud
    Hast rear'd God's trophies, and his work pursu'd,
    While Darwen stream with blood of Scots imbru'd,
    And Dunbar field, resounds thy praises loud,
And Worcester's laureate wreath; yet much remains
    To conquer still: peace hath her victories
    No less renown'd than war. New foes arise
Threat'ning to bind our souls with secular chains:
    Help us to save free Conscience from the paw
    Of hireling wolves whose gospel is their maw.

Lycidas

Yet once more, O ye laurels, and once more
Ye myrtles brown, with ivy never sere,
I come to pluck your berries harsh and crude,
And with forc'd fingers rude
Shatter your leaves before the mellowing year.
Bitter constraint and sad occasion dear
Compels me to disturb your season due;

For Lycidas is dead, dead ere his prime,
Young Lycidas, and hath not left his peer.
Who would not sing for Lycidas? he knew
Himself to sing, and build the lofty rhyme.
He must not float upon his wat'ry bier
Unwept, and welter to the parching wind,
Without the meed of some melodious tear.

Begin then, Sisters of the sacred well
That from beneath the seat of Jove doth spring;
Begin, and somewhat loudly sweep the string.
Hence with denial vain and coy excuse!
So may some gentle muse
With lucky words favour my destin'd urn,
And as he passes turn
And bid fair peace be to my sable shroud!

For we were nurs'd upon the self-same hill,
Fed the same flock, by fountain, shade, and rill;
Together both, ere the high lawns appear'd
Under the opening eyelids of the morn,
We drove afield, and both together heard
What time the gray-fly winds her sultry horn,
Batt'ning our flocks with the fresh dews of night,
Oft till the star that rose at ev'ning bright
Toward heav'n's descent had slop'd his westering wheel.
Meanwhile the rural ditties were not mute,
Temper'd to th'oaten flute;
Rough Satyrs danc'd, and Fauns with clov'n heel,
From the glad sound would not be absent long;
And old Damætas lov'd to hear our song.

But O the heavy change now thou art gone,
Now thou art gone, and never must return!
Thee, Shepherd, thee the woods and desert caves,

With wild thyme and the gadding vine o'ergrown,
And all their echoes mourn.
The willows and the hazel copses green
Shall now no more be seen
Fanning their joyous leaves to thy soft lays.
As killing as the canker to the rose,
Or taint-worm to the weanling herds that graze,
Or frost to flowers that their gay wardrobe wear
When first the white thorn blows:
Such, Lycidas, thy loss to shepherd's ear.

Where were ye, Nymphs, when the remorseless deep
Clos'd o'er the head of your lov'd Lycidas?
For neither were ye playing on the steep
Where your old bards, the famous Druids, lie,
Nor on the shaggy top of Mona high,
Nor yet where Deva spreads her wizard stream.
Ay me! I fondly dream
Had ye bin there'—for what could that have done?
What could the Muse herself that Orpheus bore,
The Muse herself, for her enchanting son,
Whom universal nature did lament,
When by the rout that made the hideous roar
His gory visage down the stream was sent,
Down the swift Hebrus to the Lesbian shore?

Alas! what boots it with incessant care
To tend the homely, slighted shepherd's trade,
And strictly meditate the thankless Muse?
Were it not better done, as others use,
To sport with Amaryllis in the shade,
Or with the tangles of Neæra's hair?
Fame is the spur that the clear spirit doth raise
(That last infirmity of noble mind)
To scorn delights and live laborious days;

But the fair guerdon when we hope to find,
And think to burst out into sudden blaze,
Comes the blind Fury with th'abhorred shears,
And slits the thin-spun life. "But not the praise,"
Phoebus replied, and touch'd my trembling ears;
"Fame is no plant that grows on mortal soil,
Nor in the glistering foil
Set off to th'world, nor in broad rumour lies,
But lives and spreads aloft by those pure eyes
And perfect witness of all-judging Jove;
As he pronounces lastly on each deed,
Of so much fame in Heav'n expect thy meed."

O fountain Arethuse, and thou honour'd flood,
Smooth-sliding Mincius, crown'd with vocal reeds,
That strain I heard was of a higher mood.
But now my oat proceeds,
And listens to the Herald of the Sea,
That came in Neptune's plea.
He ask'd the waves, and ask'd the felon winds,
"What hard mishap hath doom'd this gentle swain?"
And question'd every gust of rugged wings
That blows from off each beaked promontory.
They knew not of his story;
And sage Hippotades their answer brings,
That not a blast was from his dungeon stray'd;
The air was calm, and on the level brine
Sleek Panope with all her sisters play'd.
It was that fatal and perfidious bark,
Built in th'eclipse, and rigg'd with curses dark,
That sunk so low that sacred head of thine.

Next Camus, reverend sire, went footing slow,
His mantle hairy, and his bonnet sedge,
Inwrought with figures dim, and on the edge

Like to that sanguine flower inscrib'd with woe.
"Ah! who hath reft," quoth he, "my dearest pledge?"
Last came, and last did go,
The Pilot of the Galilean lake;
Two massy keys he bore of metals twain
(The golden opes, the iron shuts amain).
He shook his mitred locks, and stern bespake:
"How well could I have spar'd for thee, young swain,
Enow of such as for their bellies' sake
Creep and intrude, and climb into the fold?
Of other care they little reck'ning make
Than how to scramble at the shearers' feast
And shove away the worthy bidden guest.
Blind mouths! that scarce themselves know how to hold
A sheep-hook, or have learn'd aught else the least
That to the faithful herdman's art belongs!
What recks it them? What need they? They are sped;
And when they list their lean and flashy songs
Grate on their scrannel pipes of wretched straw,
The hungry sheep look up, and are not fed,
But, swoll'n with wind and the rank mist they draw,
Rot inwardly, and foul contagion spread;
Besides what the grim wolf with privy paw
Daily devours apace, and nothing said,
But that two-handed engine at the door
Stands ready to smite once, and smite no more".

Return, Alpheus: the dread voice is past
That shrunk thy streams; return, Sicilian Muse,
And call the vales and bid them hither cast
Their bells and flow'rets of a thousand hues.
Ye valleys low, where the mild whispers use
Of shades and wanton winds, and gushing brooks,
On whose fresh lap the swart star sparely looks,
Throw hither all your quaint enamel'd eyes,

That on the green turf suck the honied showers
And purple all the ground with vernal flowers.
Bring the rathe primrose that forsaken dies,
The tufted crow-toe, and pale jessamine,
The white pink, and the pansy freak'd with jet,
The glowing violet,
The musk-rose, and the well attir'd woodbine,
With cowslips wan that hang the pensive head,
And every flower that sad embroidery wears;
Bid amaranthus all his beauty shed,
And daffadillies fill their cups with tears,
To strew the laureate hearse where Lycid lies.
For so to interpose a little ease,
Let our frail thoughts dally with false surmise.
Ay me! Whilst thee the shores and sounding seas
Wash far away, where'er thy bones are hurl'd;
Whether beyond the stormy Hebrides,
Where thou perhaps under the whelming tide
Visit'st the bottom of the monstrous world,
Or whether thou, to our moist vows denied,
Sleep'st by the fable of Bellerus old,
Where the great vision of the guarded mount
Looks toward Namancos and Bayona's hold:
Look homeward Angel now, and melt with ruth:
And, O ye dolphins, waft the hapless youth.

Weep no more, woeful shepherds, weep no more,
For Lycidas, your sorrow, is not dead,
Sunk though he be beneath the wat'ry floor;
So sinks the day-star in the ocean bed,
And yet anon repairs his drooping head,
And tricks his beams, and with new spangled ore
Flames in the forehead of the morning sky:
So Lycidas sunk low, but mounted high
Through the dear might of him that walk'd the waves;

Where, other groves and other streams along,
With nectar pure his oozy locks he laves,
And hears the unexpressive nuptial song,
In the blest kingdoms meek of joy and love.
There entertain him all the Saints above,
In solemn troops, and sweet societies,
That sing, and singing in their glory move,
And wipe the tears for ever from his eyes.
Now, Lycidas, the shepherds weep no more:
Henceforth thou art the Genius of the shore,
In thy large recompense, and shalt be good
To all that wander in that perilous flood.

　　Thus sang the uncouth swain to th'oaks and rills,
While the still morn went out with sandals gray;
He touch'd the tender stops of various quills,
With eager thought warbling his Doric lay;
And now the sun had stretch'd out all the hills,
And now was dropp'd into the western bay;
At last he rose, and twitch'd his mantle blue:
To-morrow to fresh woods, and pastures new.

Dryden, John (1631-1700)

Trinity College

A rarity for a Cambridge Poet, he obtained his degree! Although in his early life he was raised as a puritan, he became the greatest poet and playwright of the Restoration and was made Poet Laureate in 1668. He was an early member of the Royal Society, dedicated to the research and expansion of scientific knowledge; he was expelled for the non-payment of dues.

He argued with another Cambridge poet, Thomas Shadwell, writing the satirical poem 'Mac Flecknoe' accusing Shadwell of dullness:

"All arguments but most his plays persuade,
That for anointed dullness he was made".

Happy the Man

Happy the man, and happy he alone,
He who can call today his own:
He who, secure within, can say,
Tomorrow do thy worst, for I have lived today.
Be fair or foul or rain or shine
The joys I have possessed, in spite of fate, are mine.

Not Heaven itself upon the past has power,
But what has been, has been, and I have had my hour.

You charm'd me not with that fair face

You charm'd me not with that fair face
    Though it was all divine:
To be another's is the grace,
    That makes me wish you mine.
  The Gods and Fortune take their part
    Who like young monarchs fight;
And boldly dare invade that heart
    Which is another's right.

  First mad with hope we undertake
    To pull up every bar;
But once possess'd, we faintly make
    A dull defensive war.

  Now every friend is turn'd a foe
    In hope to get our store:
And passion makes us cowards grow,
    Which made us brave before.

Calm was the even, and clear was the sky

Calm was the even, and clear was the sky
    And the new budding flowers did spring,
When all alone went Amyntas and I
    To hear the sweet nightingale sing;
I sate, and he laid him down by me;
    But scarcely his breath he could draw;
For when with a fear, he began to draw near,
    He was dash'd with A ha ha ha ha!

He blush'd to himself, and lay still for a while,
    And his modesty curb'd his desire;
But straight I convinc'd all his fear with a smile,
    Which added new flames to his fire.
O Silvia, said he, you are cruel,
    To keep your poor lover in awe;
Then once more he press'd with his hand to my breast,
    But was dash'd with A ha ha ha ha!

I knew 'twas his passion that caus'd all his fear;
    And therefore I pitied his case:
I whisper'd him softly, there's nobody near,
    And laid my cheek close to his face:
But as he grew bolder and bolder,
    A shepherd came by us and saw;
And just as our bliss we began with a kiss,
    He laugh'd out with A ha ha ha ha!

Thomas Shadwell (1642-1692)

Gonville and Caius College

Born in Norfolk. He entered Gonville and Caius in 1656; he left without taking a degree. A prolific playwright of moralistic bawdy comedies. He had a major falling out with Dryden, a very common practise of the time, who described him as –

> "The rest to some faint meaning make pretense,
> But Sh____ never deviates into sense."

Although popular in his day, posterity has come to regard him as Dryden described him, "the king of dullness". He succeeded Dryden as Poet Laureate although it must be said more through the political machinations of the Restoration rather than talent.

Dear Pretty Youth

Dear pretty youth, unveil your eyes,
How can you sleep when I am by?
Were I with you all night to be,
Methinks I could from sleep be free.
Alas, my dear, you're cold as stone:
You must no longer lie alone.
But be with me my dear, and I in each arm
Will hug you close and keep you warm.

Love In Their Little Veins Inspires

Love in their little veins inspires
their cheerful notes, their soft desires.
While heat makes buds and blossoms spring,
those pretty couples love and sing.
But winter puts out their desire,
and half the year they want love's fire.

Love Quickly Is Pall'd

Love quickly is pall'd,
Tho' with labour 'tis gain'd;
Wine never does cloy
Tho' with ease 'tis obtain'd.
We sing while you sigh,
We laugh while you weep;
Love robs you of rest,
Wine lulls us asleep.

Nymphs And Shepherds

Nymphs and shepherds, come away.
In this grove let's sport and play,
For this is Flora's holiday,
Sacred to ease and happy love,
To dancing, to music and to poetry;
Your flocks may now securely rest
Whilst you express your jollity.
Nymphs and shepherds, come away

Gray, Thomas (1716-1771)

Pembroke College

Studied at Peterhouse and left without taking a degree, later becoming a fellow of Pembroke. He spent most of his life as a Don at Cambridge taking little interest in the business of the University. Instead he spent his time, reading, studying and writing. In 1757 he was offered and refused the post of Poet Laureate. He died in his rooms at Pembroke.

Elegy Written in a Country Churchyard

The curfew tolls the knell of parting day,
    The lowing herd wind slowly o'er the lea,
The plowman homeward plods his weary way,
    And leaves the world to darkness and to me.

Now fades the glimm'ring landscape on the sight,
    And all the air a solemn stillness holds,
Save where the beetle wheels his droning flight,
    And drowsy tinklings lull the distant folds;

Save that from yonder ivy-mantled tow'r
    The moping owl does to the moon complain
Of such, as wand'ring near her secret bow'r,
    Molest her ancient solitary reign.

Beneath those rugged elms, that yew-tree's shade,
　　Where heaves the turf in many a mould'ring heap,
Each in his narrow cell for ever laid,
　　The rude forefathers of the hamlet sleep.

The breezy call of incense-breathing Morn,
　　The swallow twitt'ring from the straw-built shed,
The cock's shrill clarion, or the echoing horn,
　　No more shall rouse them from their lowly bed.

For them no more the blazing hearth shall burn,
　　Or busy housewife ply her evening care:
No children run to lisp their sire's return,
　　Or climb his knees the envied kiss to share.

Oft did the harvest to their sickle yield,
　　Their furrow oft the stubborn glebe has broke;
How jocund did they drive their team afield!
　　How bow'd the woods beneath their sturdy stroke!

Let not Ambition mock their useful toil,
　　Their homely joys, and destiny obscure;
Nor Grandeur hear with a disdainful smile
　　The short and simple annals of the poor.

The boast of heraldry, the pomp of pow'r,
　　And all that beauty, all that wealth e'er gave,
Awaits alike th' inevitable hour.
　　The paths of glory lead but to the grave.

Nor you, ye proud, impute to these the fault,
　　If Mem'ry o'er their tomb no trophies raise,
Where thro' the long-drawn aisle and fretted vault
　　The pealing anthem swells the note of praise.

Can storied urn or animated bust
    Back to its mansion call the fleeting breath?
Can Honour's voice provoke the silent dust,
    Or Flatt'ry soothe the dull cold ear of Death?

Perhaps in this neglected spot is laid
    Some heart once pregnant with celestial fire;
Hands, that the rod of empire might have sway'd,
    Or wak'd to ecstasy the living lyre.

But Knowledge to their eyes her ample page
    Rich with the spoils of time did ne'er unroll;
Chill Penury repress'd their noble rage,
    And froze the genial current of the soul.

Full many a gem of purest ray serene,
    The dark unfathom'd caves of ocean bear:
Full many a flow'r is born to blush unseen,
    And waste its sweetness on the desert air.

Some village-Hampden, that with dauntless breast
    The little tyrant of his fields withstood;
Some mute inglorious Milton here may rest,
    Some Cromwell guiltless of his country's blood.

Th' applause of list'ning senates to command,
    The threats of pain and ruin to despise,
To scatter plenty o'er a smiling land,
    And read their hist'ry in a nation's eyes,

Their lot forbade: nor circumscrib'd alone
    Their growing virtues, but their crimes confin'd;
Forbade to wade through slaughter to a throne,
    And shut the gates of mercy on mankind,

The struggling pangs of conscious truth to hide,
    To quench the blushes of ingenuous shame,
Or heap the shrine of Luxury and Pride
    With incense kindled at the Muse's flame.

Far from the madding crowd's ignoble strife,
    Their sober wishes never learn'd to stray;
Along the cool sequester'd vale of life
    They kept the noiseless tenor of their way.

Yet ev'n these bones from insult to protect,
    Some frail memorial still erected nigh,
With uncouth rhymes and shapeless sculpture deck'd,
    Implores the passing tribute of a sigh.

Their name, their years, spelt by th' unletter'd muse,
    The place of fame and elegy supply:
And many a holy text around she strews,
    That teach the rustic moralist to die.

For who to dumb Forgetfulness a prey,
    This pleasing anxious being e'er resign'd,
Left the warm precincts of the cheerful day,
    Nor cast one longing, ling'ring look behind?

On some fond breast the parting soul relies,
    Some pious drops the closing eye requires;
Ev'n from the tomb the voice of Nature cries,
    Ev'n in our ashes live their wonted fires.

For thee, who mindful of th' unhonour'd Dead
    Dost in these lines their artless tale relate;
If chance, by lonely contemplation led,
    Some kindred spirit shall inquire thy fate,

Haply some hoary-headed swain may say,
      "Oft have we seen him at the peep of dawn
Brushing with hasty steps the dews away
      To meet the sun upon the upland lawn.

"There at the foot of yonder nodding beech
      That wreathes its old fantastic roots so high,
His listless length at noontide would he stretch,
      And pore upon the brook that babbles by.

"Hard by yon wood, now smiling as in scorn,
      Mutt'ring his wayward fancies he would rove,
Now drooping, woeful wan, like one forlorn,
      Or craz'd with care, or cross'd in hopeless love.

"One morn I miss'd him on the custom'd hill,
      Along the heath and near his fav'rite tree;
Another came; nor yet beside the rill,
      Nor up the lawn, nor at the wood was he;

"The next with dirges due in sad array
      Slow thro' the church-way path we saw him borne.
Approach and read (for thou canst read) the lay,
      Grav'd on the stone beneath yon aged thorn."

The Epitaph

Here rests his head upon the lap of Earth
      A youth to Fortune and to Fame unknown.
Fair Science frown'd not on his humble birth,
      And Melancholy mark'd him for her own.
Large was his bounty, and his soul sincere,
      Heav'n did a recompense as largely send:

He gave to Mis'ry all he had, a tear,
    He gain'd from Heav'n ('twas all he wish'd) a friend.
No farther seek his merits to disclose,
    Or draw his frailties from their dread abode,
(There they alike in trembling hope repose)
    The bosom of his Father and his God.

Wordsworth, William (1770-1850)

St John's College

He received his degree but disliked the academic course. One of the great English poets and alongside Coleridge one of the founders of Romanticism. He was later derided by other Romantic poets, such as Byron and Shelley, for giving up his youthful ideals. In 1843 he became Poet Laureate.

Inside of King's College Chapel, Cambridge

Tax not the royal Saint with vain expense,
With ill-matched aims the Architect who planned—
Albeit labouring for a scanty band
Of white-robed Scholars only—this immense
And glorious Work of fine intelligence!
Give all thou canst; high Heaven rejects the lore
Of nicely-calculated less or more;
So deemed the man who fashioned for the sense
These lofty pillars, spread that branching roof
Self-poised, and scooped into ten thousand cells,
Where light and shade repose, where music dwells
Lingering—and wandering on as loth to die;
Like thoughts whose very sweetness yieldeth proof
That they were born for immortality.

Cambridge

It was a dreary morning when the wheels
Rolled over a wide plain o'erhung with clouds,
And nothing cheered our way till first we saw
The long-roofed chapel of King's College lift
Turrets and pinnacles in answering files,
Extended high above a dusky grove.
Advancing, we espied upon the road
A student clothed in gown and tasseled cap,
Striding along as if o'ertasked by Time,
Or covetous of exercise and air;
He passed,—nor was I master of my eyes
Till he was left an arrow's flight behind.
As near and nearer to the spot we drew,
It seemed to suck us in with an eddy's force.
Onward we drove beneath the castle; caught,
While crossing Magdalene Bridge, a glimpse of Cam;
And at the Hoop alighted, famous inn.

The Evangelist St. John my patron was:
Three Gothic courts are his, and in the first
Was my abiding-place, a nook obscure;
Right underneath, the college kitchens made
A humming sound less tunable than bees,
But hardly less industrious; with shrill notes
Of sharp command and scolding intermixed.
Near me hung Trinity's loquacious clock,
Who never let the quarters, night or day,
Slip by him unproclaimed, and told the hours
Twice over with a male and female voice.
Her pealing organ was my neighbour too;
And from my pillow, looking forth by light
Of moon or favouring stars, I could behold
The antechapel where the statue stood

Of Newton, with his prism and silent face.
The marble index of a mind forever
Voyaging through strange seas of thought, alone.

All winter long, whenever free to choose,
Did I by night frequent the college groves
And tributary walks; the last, and oft
The only one, who had been lingering there
Through hours of silence, till the porter's bell,
A punctual follower on the stroke of nine,
Rang, with its blunt, unceremonious voice,
Inexorable summons! Lofty elms,
Inviting shades of opportune recess,
Bestowed composure on a neighbourhood
Unpeaceful in itself. A single tree.
With sinuous trunk, boughs exquisitely wreathed
Grew there; an ash which winter for himself
Decked as in pride, and with outlandish grace:
Up from the ground, and almost to the top,
The trunk and every master branch were green
"With clustering ivy, and the lightsome twigs
And outer spray profusely tipped with seeds
That hung in yellow tassels, while the air
Stirred them, not voiceless. Often have I stood
Foot-bound, uplooking at this lovely tree
Beneath a frosty moon. The hemisphere
Of magic fiction verse of mine perchance
May never tread: but scarcely Spenser's self
Could have more tranquil visions in his youth,
Or could more bright appearance create
Of human forms with superhuman powers,
Than I beheld, loitering on calm, clear nights,
Alone, beneath this fairy work of earth.

I Wandered Lonely as a Cloud

I wandered lonely as a cloud
That floats on high o'er vales and hills,
When all at once I saw a crowd,
A host, of golden daffodils;
Beside the lake, beneath the trees,
Fluttering and dancing in the breeze.

Continuous as the stars that shine
And twinkle on the milky way,
They stretched in never-ending line
Along the margin of a bay:
Ten thousand saw I at a glance,
Tossing their heads in sprightly dance.

The waves beside them danced; but they
Out-did the sparkling waves in glee:
A poet could not but be gay,
In such a jocund company:
I gazed—and gazed—but little thought
What wealth the show to me had brought:

For oft, when on my couch I lie
In vacant or in pensive mood,
They flash upon that inward eye
Which is the bliss of solitude;
And then my heart with pleasure fills,
And dances with the daffodils.

The Green Linnet

Beneath these fruit-tree boughs that shed
Their snow-white blossoms on my head,
With brightest sunshine round me spread
    Of spring's unclouded weather,
In this sequestered nook how sweet
To sit upon my orchard-seat!
And birds and flowers once more to greet,
    My last year's friends together.

One have I marked, the happiest guest
In all this covert of the blest:
Hail to Thee, far above the rest
    In joy of voice and pinion!
Thou, Linnet! in thy green array,
Presiding Spirit here to-day,
Dost lead the revels of the May;
    And this is thy dominion.

While birds, and butterflies, and flowers,
Make all one band of paramours,
Thou, ranging up and down the bowers,
    Art sole in thy employment:
A Life, a Presence like the Air,
Scattering thy gladness without care,
Too blest with any one to pair;
    Thyself thy own enjoyment.

Amid yon tuft of hazel trees,
That twinkle to the gusty breeze,
Behold him perched in ecstasies,
    Yet seeming still to hover;
There! where the flutter of his wings
Upon his back and body flings
Shadows and sunny glimmerings,
    That cover him all over.

My dazzled sight he oft deceives,
A brother of the dancing leaves;
Then flits, and from the cottage-eaves
    Pours forth his song in gushes;
As if by that exulting strain
He mocked and treated with disdain
The voiceless Form he chose to feign,
    While fluttering in the bushes.

To the Cuckoo

O blithe New-comer! I have heard,
I hear thee and rejoice.
O Cuckoo! shall I call thee Bird,
Or but a wandering Voice?

While I am lying on the grass
Thy twofold shout I hear;
From hill to hill it seems to pass,
At once far off, and near.

Though babbling only to the Vale
Of sunshine and of flowers,
Thou bringest unto me a tale
Of visionary hours.

Thrice welcome, darling of the Spring!
Even yet thou art to me
No bird, but an invisible thing,
A voice, a mystery;

The same whom in my school-boy days
I listened to; that Cry
Which made me look a thousand ways
In bush, and tree, and sky.

To seek thee did I often rove
Through woods and on the green;
And thou wert still a hope, a love;
Still longed for, never seen.

And I can listen to thee yet;
Can lie upon the plain
And listen, till I do beget
That golden time again.

O blessèd Bird! the earth we pace
Again appears to be
An unsubstantial, faery place;
That is fit home for Thee!

Coleridge, Samuel Taylor (1772-1834)

Jesus College

One of England's greatest poets. He came up to Cambridge in 1791. His promising academic career was sidelined by his interest in politics, heavy drinking and the accumulation of debts. Debts that became so severe that he enlisted in the 15th Light Dragoons under an assumed name. He was apparently discharged after repeatedly falling off his horse.

He, like a great many of these poets, never received a degree. An opium addict, he wrote 'Kubla Khan' whilst under the influence, a composition interrupted by a caller from the town of Porlock. Along with Wordsworth he wrote *Lyrical Ballads*, a book which redefined the world of poetry and helped to give rise to Romanticism. It is mainly due to his work as a critic that Shakespeare was rescued from obscurity.

Frost at Midnight

The Frost performs its secret ministry,
Unhelped by any wind. The owlet's cry
Came loud—and hark, again! loud as before.
The inmates of my cottage, all at rest,
Have left me to that solitude, which suits
Abstruser musings: save that at my side
My cradled infant slumbers peacefully.

'Tis calm indeed! so calm, that it disturbs
And vexes meditation with its strange
And extreme silentness. Sea, hill, and wood,
This populous village! Sea, and hill, and wood,
With all the numberless goings-on of life,

Inaudible as dreams! the thin blue flame
Lies on my low-burnt fire, and quivers not;
Only that film, which fluttered on the grate,
Still flutters there, the sole unquiet thing.
Methinks, its motion in this hush of nature
Gives it dim sympathies with me who live,
Making it a companionable form,
Whose puny flaps and freaks the idling Spirit
By its own moods interprets, every where
Echo or mirror seeking of itself,
And makes a toy of Thought.

        But O! how oft,
How oft, at school, with most believing mind,
Presageful, have I gazed upon the bars,
To watch that fluttering stranger ! and as oft
With unclosed lids, already had I dreamt
Of my sweet birth-place, and the old church-tower,
Whose bells, the poor man's only music, rang
From morn to evening, all the hot Fair-day,
So sweetly, that they stirred and haunted me
With a wild pleasure, falling on mine ear
Most like articulate sounds of things to come!
So gazed I, till the soothing things, I dreamt,
Lulled me to sleep, and sleep prolonged my dreams!
And so I brooded all the following morn,
Awed by the stern preceptor's face, mine eye
Fixed with mock study on my swimming book:
Save if the door half opened, and I snatched
A hasty glance, and still my heart leaped up,

For still I hoped to see the stranger's face,
Townsman, or aunt, or sister more beloved,
My play-mate when we both were clothed alike!

      Dear Babe, that sleepest cradled by my side,
Whose gentle breathings, heard in this deep calm,
Fill up the intersperséd vacancies
And momentary pauses of the thought!
My babe so beautiful! it thrills my heart
With tender gladness, thus to look at thee,
And think that thou shalt learn far other lore,
And in far other scenes! For I was reared
In the great city, pent 'mid cloisters dim,
And saw nought lovely but the sky and stars.
But thou, my babe! shalt wander like a breeze
By lakes and sandy shores, beneath the crags
Of ancient mountain, and beneath the clouds,
Which image in their bulk both lakes and shores
And mountain crags: so shalt thou see and hear
The lovely shapes and sounds intelligible
Of that eternal language, which thy God
Utters, who from eternity doth teach
Himself in all, and all things in himself.
Great universal Teacher! he shall mould
Thy spirit, and by giving make it ask.

Therefore all seasons shall be sweet to thee,
Whether the summer clothe the general earth
With greenness, or the redbreast sit and sing
Betwixt the tufts of snow on the bare branch
Of mossy apple-tree, while the nigh thatch
Smokes in the sun-thaw; whether the eave-drops fall
Heard only in the trances of the blast,
Or if the secret ministry of frost

Shall hang them up in silent icicles,
Quietly shining to the quiet Moon.

Desire

Where true Love burns Desire is Love's pure flame;
It is the reflex of our earthly frame,
That takes its meaning from the nobler part,
And but translates the language of the heart.

Kubla Khan

In Xanadu did Kubla Khan
A stately pleasure-dome decree:
Where Alph, the sacred river, ran
Through caverns measureless to man
    Down to a sunless sea.
So twice five miles of fertile ground
With walls and towers were girdled round;
And there were gardens bright with sinuous rills,
Where blossomed many an incense-bearing tree;
And here were forests ancient as the hills,
Enfolding sunny spots of greenery.

But oh! that deep romantic chasm which slanted
Down the green hill athwart a cedarn cover!
A savage place! as holy and enchanted
As e'er beneath a waning moon was haunted
By woman wailing for her demon-lover!
And from this chasm, with ceaseless turmoil seething,
As if this earth in fast thick pants were breathing,
A mighty fountain momently was forced:
Amid whose swift half-intermitted burst
Huge fragments vaulted like rebounding hail,
Or chaffy grain beneath the thresher's flail:
And mid these dancing rocks at once and ever
It flung up momently the sacred river.
Five miles meandering with a mazy motion
Through wood and dale the sacred river ran,
Then reached the caverns measureless to man,
And sank in tumult to a lifeless ocean;
And 'mid this tumult Kubla heard from far
Ancestral voices prophesying war!
 The shadow of the dome of pleasure
 Floated midway on the waves;
 Where was heard the mingled measure
 From the fountain and the caves.
It was a miracle of rare device,
A sunny pleasure-dome with caves of ice!

 A damsel with a dulcimer
 In a vision once I saw:
 It was an Abyssinian maid
 And on her dulcimer she played,
 Singing of Mount Abora.
 Could I revive within me
 Her symphony and song,
 To such a deep delight 'twould win me,

That with music loud and long,
I would build that dome in air,
That sunny dome! those caves of ice!
And all who heard should see them there,
And all should cry, Beware! Beware!
His flashing eyes, his floating hair!
Weave a circle round him thrice,
And close your eyes with holy dread
For he on honey-dew hath fed,
And drunk the milk of Paradise.

Byron, George Gordon Lord (1788-1824)

Trinity College

It is difficult to know where to begin with Byron, a man who died at the early age of thirty-six and yet filled his life with genius, scandal, poetry and women. Described by Lady Caroline Lamb, one of his spurned lovers, as "mad, bad and dangerous to know", although she wasn't exactly a beacon of sanity herself.

He described Trinity as "a villainous chaos of din and drunkenness". It wasn't long before he upheld this great tradition, reputedly keeping a bear in his rooms. The college rules forbad the keeping of a dog. He left England in 1816 never to return because of rising debts and rising scandal, among them allegations of incest and sodomy.

An interesting man, to say the least. In no particular order: he had a club foot, weight issues (he spent much of his life on a vegetarian diet, possibly bulimic), curled his hair, was probably bisexual, his father was known as 'Mad Jack' which is never a good start in life, he was a lover of animals, he wished to be buried with his dog 'boatswain', spoke Armenian, swam the Hellespont, became an adjective, had three children (approx.) by three different women – one of them his sister.

He died of a fever in April 1824 while fighting for Greek independence and is remembered as a Greek national hero.

After his death his friends commissioned a statue of Byron which they proposed should be erected in Poets' corner at

Westminster Abbey, but such was his reputation that the Abbey refused. It is now in the Wren Library at Trinity. In 1969 (145 years after his death) a statue was erected in Westminster.

She Walks in Beauty

She walks in beauty, like the night
   Of cloudless climes and starry skies;
And all that's best of dark and bright
   Meet in her aspect and her eyes;
Thus mellowed to that tender light
   Which heaven to gaudy day denies.

One shade the more, one ray the less,
   Had half impaired the nameless grace
Which waves in every raven tress,
   Or softly lightens o'er her face;
Where thoughts serenely sweet express,
   How pure, how dear their dwelling-place.

And on that cheek, and o'er that brow,
   So soft, so calm, yet eloquent,
The smiles that win, the tints that glow,
   But tell of days in goodness spent,
A mind at peace with all below,
   A heart whose love is innocent!

So We'll Go No More a Roving

So, we'll go no more a roving
   So late into the night,
Though the heart be still as loving,
   And the moon be still as bright.

For the sword outwears its sheath,
   And the soul wears out the breast,
And the heart must pause to breathe,
   And love itself have rest.

Though the night was made for loving,
   And the day returns too soon,
Yet we'll go no more a roving
   By the light of the moon.

Milnes, Richard (1809-1885)

Trinity College

1st Baron Houghton. A member of the Cambridge Apostles, which at the time included Alfred Lord Tennyson. He later became a Conservative member of parliament. A minor poet and long-time suitor of Florence Nightingale. After his death he left a huge collection of erotic literature to the British Library.

On revisiting Trinity College, Cambridge

I have a debt of my heart's own to thee,
School of my soul! old lime and cloister shade!
Which I, strange suitor, should lament to see
Fully acquitted and exactly paid.
The first ripe taste of manhood's best delights,
Knowledge imbibed, while mind and heart agree,
In sweet belated talk on winter nights,
"With friends whom growing time keeps dear to me;—
Such things I owe thee, and not only these:
I owe thee the far-beaconing memories
Of the young dead, who, having crossed the tide
Of Life where it was narrow, deep, and clear,
Now cast their brightness from the farther side
On the dark-flowing hours I breast in fear.

Tennyson, Alfred Lord (1809-1892)

Trinity College

The most popular poet of his day. A member of the Cambridge Apostles. He was awarded the Chancellor's Gold medal for one of his early poems 'Timbuctoo'. After the death of his father he had to leave Cambridge without taking his degree. He was made Poet Laureate in 1850, a post he held until his death.

Trinity

I past beside the reverend walls
In which of old I wore the gown;
I roved at random through the town,
And saw the tumult of the halls;
And heard once more in college fanes
The storm their high-built organs make,
And thunder-music, rolling, shake
The prophets blazoned on the panes;
And caught once more the distant shout,
The measured pulse of racing oars
Among the willows; paced the shores
And many a bridge, and all about
The same gray flats again, and felt
The same, but not the same; and last

Up that long walk of limes I past
To see the rooms in which he dwelt.
Another name was on the door:
I lingered; all within was noise
Of songs, and clapping hands, and boys
That crashed the glass and beat the floor;
Where once we held debate, a band
Of youthful friends, on mind and art
And labour, and the changing mart,
And all the framework of the land;
When one would aim an arrow fair.
But send it slackly from the string;
And one would pierce an outer ring,
And one an inner, here and there;
And last the master-bowman, he
Would cleave the mark. A willing ear
We lent him. Who, but hung to hear
The wrapt oration flowing free
From point to point with power and grace,
And music in the bounds of law,
To those conclusions when we saw
The God within him light his face,
And seem to lift the form, and glow
In azure orbits heavenly-wise;
And over those ethereal eyes
The bar of Michael Angelo.

The Eagle

He clasps the crag with crooked hands;
Close to the sun in lonely lands,
Ring'd with the azure world, he stands.

The wrinkled sea beneath him crawls;
He watches from his mountain walls,
And like a thunderbolt he falls.

Mariana

"Mariana in the Moated Grange"
(Shakespeare, Measure for Measure)

With blackest moss the flower-plots
    Were thickly crusted, one and all:
The rusted nails fell from the knots
    That held the pear to the gable-wall.
The broken sheds look'd sad and strange:
    Unlifted was the clinking latch;
    Weeded and worn the ancient thatch
Upon the lonely moated grange.
        She only said, "My life is dreary,
            He cometh not," she said;
        She said, "I am aweary, aweary,
            I would that I were dead!"

Her tears fell with the dews at even;
    Her tears fell ere the dews were dried;
She could not look on the sweet heaven,
    Either at morn or eventide.
After the flitting of the bats,
    When thickest dark did trance the sky,

She drew her casement-curtain by,
And glanced athwart the glooming flats.
      She only said, "The night is dreary,
            He cometh not," she said;
      She said, "I am aweary, aweary,
            I would that I were dead!"

Upon the middle of the night,
      Waking she heard the night-fowl crow:
The cock sung out an hour ere light:
      From the dark fen the oxen's low
Came to her: without hope of change,
      In sleep she seem'd to walk forlorn,
      Till cold winds woke the gray-eyed morn
About the lonely moated grange.
      She only said, "The day is dreary,
            He cometh not," she said;
      She said, "I am aweary, aweary,
            I would that I were dead!"

About a stone-cast from the wall
      A sluice with blacken'd waters slept,
And o'er it many, round and small,
      The cluster'd marish-mosses crept.
Hard by a poplar shook alway,
      All silver-green with gnarled bark:
      For leagues no other tree did mark
The level waste, the rounding gray.
      She only said, "My life is dreary,
            He cometh not," she said;
      She said "I am aweary, aweary
            I would that I were dead!"

And ever when the moon was low,
      And the shrill winds were up and away,
In the white curtain, to and fro,

She saw the gusty shadow sway.
But when the moon was very low
  And wild winds bound within their cell,
  The shadow of the poplar fell
Upon her bed, across her brow.
    She only said, "The night is dreary,
      He cometh not," she said;
    She said "I am aweary, aweary,
      I would that I were dead!"

All day within the dreamy house,
  The doors upon their hinges creak'd;
The blue fly sung in the pane; the mouse
  Behind the mouldering wainscot shriek'd,
Or from the crevice peer'd about.
  Old faces glimmer'd thro' the doors
  Old footsteps trod the upper floors,
Old voices called her from without.
    She only said, "My life is dreary,
      He cometh not," she said;
    She said, "I am aweary, aweary,
      I would that I were dead!"

The sparrow's chirrup on the roof,
  The slow clock ticking, and the sound
Which to the wooing wind aloof
  The poplar made, did all confound
Her sense; but most she loathed the hour
  When the thick-moted sunbeam lay
  Athwart the chambers, and the day
Was sloping toward his western bower.
    Then said she, "I am very dreary,
      He will not come," she said;
    She wept, "I am aweary, aweary,
      Oh God, that I were dead!"

Claribel

Where Claribel low-lieth
    The breezes pause and die,
    Letting the rose-leaves fall:
But the solemn oak-tree sigheth,
    Thick-leaved, ambrosial,
    With an ancient melody
    Of an inward agony,
Where Claribel low-lieth.

At eve the beetle boometh
    Athwart the thicket lone:
At noon the wild bee hummeth
    About the moss'd headstone:
At midnight the moon cometh,
    And looketh down alone.
Her song the lintwhite swelleth,
The clear-voiced mavis dwelleth,
    The callow throstle lispeth,
The slumbrous wave outwelleth,
    The babbling runnel crispeth,
The hollow grot replieth
    Where Claribel low-lieth.

FitzGerald, Edward (1809-1883)

Trinity College

Famously he was the first, and some consider the best, translator of the Rubaiyat of Omar Khayyam. One of the few poets in this collection never to have been offered membership of the Cambridge Apostles. He lived a quiet life as a Bachelor, his marriage was not a success. While at Cambridge he resided at number 19 King's Parade.

'Euphranor' was written in memory of his time at Cambridge, this is a short extract:

DURING the time of my pretending to practise
Medicine at Cambridge, I was aroused, one
fine forenoon of May, by the sound of some
one coming up my staircase, two or three
steps at a time it seemed to me; then,
directly after, a smart rapping at the door;
and, before I could say, "Come in,"
Euphranor had opened it, and, striding up
to me, seized my arm with his usual eager-
ness, and told me I must go out with him—
" It was such a day—sun shining—breeze
blowing—hedges and trees in full leaf.—
He had been to Chesterton, (he said,) and
pull'd back with a man who now left him

in the lurch ; and I must take his place."
I told him what a poor hand at the oar I
was, and, such walnut-shells as these Cam-
bridge boats were, I was sure a strong fellow
like him must rejoice in getting a whole
Eight-oar to himself once in a while. He
laughed, and said, " The pace, the pace was
the thing—However, that was all nothing,
but—in short, I must go with him, whether
for a row, or a walk in the fields, or a game
of Billiards at Chesterton—whatever I liked
—only go I must." After a little more
banter, about some possible Patients, I got
up ; closed some very weary medical Treatise
I was reading; on with coat and hat; and
in three minutes we had run downstairs, out
into the open air; where both of us call-
ing out together "What a day!" it was, we
struck out briskly for the old Wooden Bridge,
where Euphranor said his boat was lying.

To a Lady Singing

Canst thou, my Clora, declare,
After thy sweet song dieth
Into the wild summer air,
Whither it falleth or flieth ?
Soon would my answer be noted,
Wert thou but sage as sweet throated.
Melody, dying away,
Into the dark sky closes,
Like the good soul from her clay
Like the fair odor of roses:
Therefore thou now art behind it,

But thou shalt follow, and find it.
Nothing can utterly die;
Music, aloft upspringing,
Turns to pure atoms of sky
Each golden note of thy singing :
And that to which morning did listen
At eve in a Rainbow may glisten.
Beauty, when laid in the grave,
Feedeth the lily beside her,
Therefore the soul cannot have
Station or honour denied her ;
She will not better her essence,
But wear a crown in God's presence

To a Violet

Fair violet! sweet saint!
Answer us—Whither art thou gone?
Ever thou wert so still, and faint,
And fearing to be look'd upon.
We cannot say that one hath died,
Who wont to live so unespied,
But crept away unto a stiller spot,
Where men may stir the grass, and find thee not.

The Meadows in Spring

'Tis a dull sight
To see the year dying,
When winter winds
Set the yellow wood sighing:
Sighing, oh! sighing.

When such a time cometh,
I do retire
Into and old room
Beside a bright fire:
Oh, pile a bright fire!

And there I sit
Reading old things,
Of knights and lorn damsels,
While the wind sings—
Oh, drearily sings!

I never look out
Nor attend to the blast;
For all to be seen
Is the leaves falling fast:
Falling, falling!

But close at the hearth,
Like a cricket, sit I,
Reading of summer
And chivalry—
Gallant chivalry!

Then with an old friend
I talk of our youth!
How 'twas gladsome, but often
Foolish, forsooth:
But gladsome, gladsome!

Or to get merry
We sing some old rhyme,
That made the wood ring again
In summertime—
Sweet summertime!

Then go we to smoking,
Silent and snug:
Nought passes between us,
Save a brown jug—
Sometimes!

And sometimes a tear
Will rise in each eye,
Seeing the two old friends
So merrily—
So merrily!

And ere to bed
Go we, go we,
Down on the ashes
We kneel on the knee,
Praying together!

Thus, then, live I,
Till, 'mid all the gloom,
By heaven! the bold sun
Is with me in the room
Shining, shining!

Then the clouds part,
Swallow soaring between;
The spring is alive,
And the meadows are green!

I jump up, like mad,
Break the old pipe in twain,
And away to the meadows,
The meadows again!

Thackeray, William Makepeace (1811-1868)

Trinity College

Born in Calcutta. Most famous for his satirical novels. During his lifetime he was second only to Dickens in popularity. It is rumoured that, while at Cambridge, Thackeray discovered a taste for gambling and alcohol. It was also here that he began his lifelong friendship with Edward FitzGerald.

"A clever, ugly man every now and then is successful with the ladies, but a handsome fool is irresistible."

The Cane-Bottom'd Chair

In tattered old slippers that toast at the bars,
And a ragged old jacket perfumed with cigars,
Away from the world and its toils and its cares,
I've a snug little kingdom up four pair of stairs.

To mount to this realm is a toil, to be sure,
But the fire there is bright and the air rather pure;
And the view I behold on a sunshiny day
Is grand through the chimney-pots over the way.

This snug little chamber is cramm'd in all nooks
With worthless old nicknacks and silly old books,
And foolish old odds and foolish old ends,
Crack'd bargains from brokers, cheap keepsakes from friends.

Old armour, prints, pictures, pipes, china (all crack'd),
Old rickety tables, and chairs broken-backed;
A twopenny treasury, wondrous to see;
What matter? 'tis pleasant to you, friend, and me.

No better divan need the Sultan require,
Than the creaking old sofa that basks by the fire;
And 'tis wonderful, surely, what music you get
From the rickety, ramshackle, wheezy spinet.

That praying-rug came from a Turcoman's camp;
By Tiber once twinkled that brazen old lamp;
A Mameluke fierce yonder dagger has drawn:
'Tis a murderous knife to toast muffins upon.

Long, long through the hours, and the night, and the chimes,
Here we talk of old books, and old friends, and old times;
As we sit in a fog made of rich Latakie
This chamber is pleasant to you, friend, and me.

But of all the cheap treasures that garnish my nest,
There's one that I love and I cherish the best:
For the finest of couches that's padded with hair
I never would change thee, my cane-bottom'd chair.

'Tis a bandy-legg'd, high-shoulder'd, worm-eaten seat,
With a creaking old back, and twisted old feet;
But since the fair morning when Fanny sat there,
I bless thee and love thee, old cane-bottom'd chair.

If chairs have but feeling, in holding such charms,
A thrill must have pass'd through your wither'd old arms!
I look'd, and I long'd, and I wish'd in despair;
I wish'd myself turn'd to a cane-bottom'd chair.

It was but a moment she sat in this place,
She'd a scarf on her neck, and a smile on her face!
A smile on her face, and a rose in her hair,
And she sat there, and bloom'd in my cane-bottom'd chair.

And so I have valued my chair ever since,
Like the shrine of a saint, or the throne of a prince;
Saint Fanny, my patroness sweet I declare,
The queen of my heart and my cane-bottom'd chair.

When the candles burn low, and the company's gone,
In the silence of night as I sit here alone--
I sit here alone, but we yet are a pair--
My Fanny I see in my cane-bottom'd chair.

She comes from the past and revisits my room;
She looks as she then did, all beauty and bloom;
So smiling and tender, so fresh and so fair,
And yonder she sits in my cane-bottom'd chair.

The Mahogany Tree

Christmas is here:
Winds whistle shrill,
Icy and chill,
Little care we:
Little we fear
Weather without,
Sheltered about
The Mahogany Tree.

Once on the boughs
Birds of rare plume
Sang, in its bloom;
Night-birds are we:
Here we carouse,
Singing like them,
Perched round the stem
Of the jolly old tree.

Here let us sport,
Boys, as we sit;
Laughter and wit
Flashing so free.
Life is but short--
When we are gone,
Let them sing on,
Round the old tree.

Evenings we knew,
Happy as this;
Faces we miss,
Pleasant to see.
Kind hearts and true,
Gentle and just,
Peace to your dust!
We sing round the tree.

Care, like a dun,
Lurks at the gate:
Let the dog wait;
Happy we'll be!
Drink, every one;
Pile up the coals,
Fill the red bowls,
Round the old tree!

Drain we the cup.--
Friend, art afraid?
Spirits are laid
In the Red Sea.
Mantle it up;
Empty it yet;
Let us forget,
Round the old tree.

Sorrows, begone!
Life and its ills,
Duns and their bills,
Bid we to flee.
Come with the dawn,
Blue-devil sprite,
Leave us to-night,
Round the old tree.

Calverley, Charles Stuart (1831-1884)

Christ's College

Came to Cambridge after being kicked out of Oxford in his second year. As the owning of dogs was forbidden, when caught walking a small brown mongrel he claimed that it was, in fact, a squirrel.

A largely forgotten poet. His work was, in the main, parodies of other poets who have themselves been forgotten (an all too familiar hazard for poets).

His Poem 'Ode to Tobacco' is on a plaque in Rose Crescent a tribute to the tobacconists which once stood upon that spot.

Ode To Tobacco

Thou, who when fears attack
Bidst them avaunt, and Black
Care, at the horseman's back
Perching, unseatest;
Sweet when the morn is gray;
Sweet when they've cleared away
Lunch; and at close of day
Possibly sweetest!

I have a liking old
For thee, though manifold
Stories, I know, are told
Not to thy credit:
How one (or two at most)
Drops make a cat a ghost,—
Useless, except to roast—
Doctors have said it;

How they who use fusees
All grow by slow degrees
Brainless as chimpanzees,
Meagre as lizards,
Go mad, and beat their wives,
Plunge (after shocking lives)
Razors and carving-knives
Into their gizzards.

Confound such knavish tricks!
Yet know I five or six
Smokers who freely mix
Still with their neighbors,—
Jones, who, I'm glad to say,
Asked leave of Mrs. J.,
Daily absorbs a clay
After his labors.

Cats may have had their goose
Cooked by tobacco juice;
Still, why deny its use
Thoughtfully taken?
We're not as tabbies are;
Smith, take a fresh cigar!
Jones, the tobacco jar!
Here's to thee, Bacon!

Ballad

The auld wife sat at her ivied door,
   (Butter and eggs and a pound of cheese)
A thing she had frequently done before;
   And her spectacles lay on her apron'd knees.

The piper he piped on the hill-top high,
   (Butter and eggs and a pound of cheese)
Till the cow said "I die," and the goose ask'd "Why?"
   And the dog said nothing, but search'd for fleas.

The farmer he strode through the square farmyard;
   (Butter and eggs and a pound of cheese)
His last brew of ale was a trifle hard -
   The connexion of which with the plot one sees.

The farmer's daughter hath frank blue eyes;
   (Butter and eggs and a pound of cheese)
She hears the rooks caw in the windy skies,
   As she sits at her lattice and shells her peas.

The farmer's daughter hath ripe red lips;
   (Butter and eggs and a pound of cheese)
If you try to approach her, away she skips
   Over tables and chairs with apparent ease.

The farmer's daughter hath soft brown hair;
   (Butter and eggs and a pound of cheese)
And I met with a ballad, I can't say where,
   Which wholly consisted of lines like these.

PART II.

She sat with her hands 'neath her dimpled cheeks,
  (Butter and eggs and a pound of cheese)
And spake not a word. While a lady speaks
  There is hope, but she didn't even sneeze.

She sat, with her hands 'neath her crimson cheeks;
  (Butter and eggs and a pound of cheese)
She gave up mending her father's breeks,
  And let the cat roll in her new chemise.

She sat, with her hands 'neath her burning cheeks,
  (Butter and eggs and a pound of cheese)
And gazed at the piper for thirteen weeks;
  Then she follow'd him out o'er the misty leas.

Her sheep follow'd her, as their tails did them.
  (Butter and eggs and a pound of cheese)
And this song is consider'd a perfect gem,
  And as to the meaning, it's what you please.

Love

Canst thou love me, lady?
  I've not learn'd to woo:
Thou art on the shady
  Side of sixty too.
Still I love thee dearly!
  Thou hast lands and pelf:
But I love thee merely
  Merely for thyself.

Wilt thou love me, fairest?
  Though thou art not fair;
And I think thou wearest
  Someone-else's hair.
Thou could'st love, though, dearly:
  And, as I am told,
Thou art very nearly
  Worth thy weight, in gold.

Dost thou love me, sweet one?
  Tell me that thou dost!
Women fairly beat one,
  But I think thou must.
Thou art loved so dearly:
  I am plain, but then
Thou (to speak sincerely)
  Art as plain again.

Love me, bashful fairy!
  I've an empty purse:
And I've "moods," which vary;
  Mostly for the worse.
Still, I love thee dearly:
  Though I make (I feel)
Love a little queerly,
  I'm as true as steel.

Love me, swear to love me
  (As, you know, they do)
By yon heaven above me
  And its changeless blue.
Love me, lady, dearly,
  If you'll be so good;
Though I don't see clearly
  On what ground you should.

Love me--ah or love me
  Not, but be my bride!
Do not simply shove me
  (So to speak) aside!
P'raps it would be dearly
  Purchased at the price;
But a hundred yearly
  Would be very nice.

"HIC VIR, HIC EST."

Often, when o'er tree and turret,
  Eve a dying radiance flings,
By that ancient pile I linger
  Known familiarly as "King's."
And the ghosts of days departed
  Rise, and in my burning breast
All the undergraduate wakens,
  And my spirit is at rest.

What, but a revolting fiction,
  Seems the actual result
Of the Census's enquiries
  Made upon the 15th ult.?
Still my soul is in its boyhood;
  Nor of year or changes recks.
Though my scalp is almost hairless,
  And my figure grows convex.

Backward moves the kindly dial;
  And I'm numbered once again
With those noblest of their species
  Called emphatically 'Men':
Loaf, as I have loafed aforetime,

Through the streets, with tranquil mind,
And a long-backed fancy-mongrel
  Trailing casually behind:

Past the Senate-house I saunter,
  Whistling with an easy grace;
Past the cabbage-stalks that carpet
  Still the beefy market-place;
Poising evermore the eye-glass
  In the light sarcastic eye,
Lest, by chance, some breezy nursemaid
  Pass, without a tribute, by.

Once, an unassuming Freshman,
  Through these wilds I wandered on,
Seeing in each house a College,
  Under every cap a Don:
Each perambulating infant
  Had a magic in its squall,
For my eager eye detected
  Senior Wranglers in them all.

By degrees my education
  Grew, and I became as others;
Learned to court delirium tremens
  By the aid of Bacon Brothers;
Bought me tiny boots of Mortlock,
  And colossal prints of Roe;
And ignored the proposition
  That both time and money go.

Learned to work the wary dogcart
  Artfully through King's Parade;
Dress, and steer a boat, and sport with
  Amaryllis in the shade:

Struck, at Brown's, the dashing hazard;
  Or (more curious sport than that)
Dropped, at Callaby's, the terrier
  Down upon the prisoned rat.

I have stood serene on Fenner's
  Ground, indifferent to blisters,
While the Buttress of the period
  Bowled me his peculiar twisters:
Sung 'We won't go home till morning';
  Striven to part my backhair straight;
Drunk (not lavishly) of Miller's
  Old dry wines at 78:-

When within my veins the blood ran,
  And the curls were on my brow,
I did, oh ye undergraduates,
  Much as ye are doing now.
Wherefore bless ye, O beloved ones:-
  Now unto mine inn must I,
Your 'poor moralist', {51a} betake me,
  In my 'solitary fly'.

Housman A.E. (1859-1936)

Trinity College

One of the greatest Classical scholars of his age, although he never studied at Cambridge. Instead he went to Oxford where he, like so many others, failed to obtain a degree, probably due to overconfidence in his abilities. However such was his erudition and reputation as an independent scholar that he eventually became Professor of Latin at University College London before becoming the Kennedy Professor of Latin at Cambridge in 1911. One of his quotes should be read by all students and scholars –

"Knowledge is good, method is good, but one thing beyond all others is necessary; and that is to have a head, not a pumpkin, on your shoulders, and brains, not pudding, in your head."

His poetry can be seen as an antidote to his learning as he believed that poetry should engage the emotions rather than the intellect.

A Shropshire Lad II: Loveliest of trees, the cherry now

Loveliest of trees, the cherry now
Is hung with bloom along the bough,
And stands about the woodland ride
Wearing white for Eastertide.

Now, of my threescore years and ten,
Twenty will not come again,
And take from seventy springs a score,
It only leaves me fifty more.

And since to look at things in bloom
Fifty springs are little room,
About the woodlands I will go
To see the cherry hung with snow.

A Shropshire Lad XXVI: Along the field as we came by

Along the field as we came by
A year ago, my love and I,
The aspen over stile and stone
Was talking to itself alone.
"Oh who are these that kiss and pass?
A country lover and his lass;
Two lovers looking to be wed;
And time shall put them both to bed,
But she shall lie with earth above,
And he beside another love."

And sure enough beneath the tree
There walks another love with me,
And overhead the aspen heaves
Its rainy-sounding silver leaves;
And I spell nothing in their stir,
But now perhaps they speak to her,
And plain for her to understand
They talk about a time at hand
When I shall sleep with clover clad,
And she beside another lad.

Is My Team Ploughing

"Is my team ploughing,
    That I was used to drive
And hear the harness jingle
    When I was man alive?"

Ay, the horses trample,
    The harness jingles now;
No change though you lie under
    The land you used to plough.

"Is football playing
    Along the river shore,
With lads to chase the leather,
    Now I stand up no more?"

Ay the ball is flying,
    The lads play heart and soul;
The goal stands up, the keeper
    Stands up to keep the goal.

"Is my girl happy,
   That I thought hard to leave,
And has she tired of weeping
   As she lies down at eve?"

Ay, she lies down lightly,
   She lies not down to weep:
Your girl is well contented.
   Be still, my lad, and sleep.

"Is my friend hearty,
   Now I am thin and pine,
And has he found to sleep in
   A better bed than mine?"

Yes, lad, I lie easy,
   I lie as lads would choose;
I cheer a dead man's sweetheart,
   Never ask me whose.

Sassoon, Siegfried (1886-1967)

Clare College

He studied History but left before obtaining a degree. He is best remembered as an anti-war poet. After receiving the Military Cross and the nickname 'Mad Jack', Sassoon wrote an open letter condemning the war, writing, "I believe that the war upon which I entered as a war of defence and liberation has now become a war of aggression and conquest".

Thrushes

Tossed on the glittering air they soar and skim,
Whose voices make the emptiness of light
A windy palace. Quavering from the brim
Of dawn, and bold with song at edge of night,
They clutch their leafy pinnacles and sing
Scornful of man, and from his toils aloof
Whose heart's a haunted woodland whispering;
Whose thoughts return on tempest-baffled wing;
Who hears the cry of God in everything,
And storms the gate of nothingness for proof.

When I'm among a blaze of lights...

When I'm among a blaze of lights,
With tawdry music and cigars
And women dawdling through delights,
And officers at cocktail bars,--
Sometimes I think of garden nights
And elm trees nodding at the stars.

I dream of a small firelit room
With yellow candles burning straight,
And glowing pictures in the gloom,
And kindly books that hold me late.
Of things like these I love to think
When I can never be alone:
Then some one says, "Another drink?"--
And turns my living heart to stone.

Everyone Sang

Everyone suddenly burst out singing;
And I was filled with such delight
As prisoned birds must find in freedom
Winging wildly across the white
Orchards and dark green fields; on; on; and out of sight.

Everyone's voice was suddenly lifted,
And beauty came like the setting sun.
My heart was shaken with tears and horror
Drifted away ... O but every one
Was a bird; and the song was wordless; the singing will never
be done.

The Redeemer

Darkness: the rain sluiced down; the mire was deep;
It was past twelve on a mid-winter night,
When peaceful folk in beds lay snug asleep;
There, with much work to do before the light,
We lugged our clay-sucked boots as best we might
Along the trench; sometimes a bullet sang,
And droning shells burst with a hollow bang;
We were soaked, chilled and wretched, every one;
Darkness; the distant wink of a huge gun.

I turned in the black ditch, loathing the storm;
A rocket fizzed and burned with blanching flare,
And lit the face of what had been a form
Floundering in mirk. He stood before me there;
I say that He was Christ; stiff in the glare,
And leaning forward from His burdening task,
Both arms supporting it; His eyes on mine
Stared from the woeful head that seemed a mask
Of mortal pain in Hell's unholy shine.
No thorny crown, only a woollen cap
He wore—an English soldier, white and strong,
Who loved his time like any simple chap,
Good days of work and sport and homely song;
Now he has learned that nights are very long,
And dawn a watching of the windowed sky.
But to the end, unjudging, he'll endure
Horror and pain, not uncontent to die
That Lancaster on Lune may stand secure.

He faced me, reeling in his weariness,
Shouldering his load of planks, so hard to bear.
I say that He was Christ, who wrought to bless
All groping things with freedom bright as air,

And with His mercy washed and made them fair.
Then the flame sank, and all grew black as pitch,
While we began to struggle along the ditch;
And someone flung his burden in the muck,
Mumbling: 'O Christ Almighty, now I'm stuck!'

Brooke, Rupert (1887-1915)

King's College

A symbol of the best that England had to offer in both body and mind. A romantic ideal in both life and especially after death. Although his atheism, socialist outlooks, possible bisexuality and a predilection for skinny dipping would have shocked contemporary society if they'd been more widely known.

He died at age twenty-seven of sepsis brought on by a mosquito bite while on route to Greece. The first of the 'war poets' to die. Having never experienced the horrors of the First World War, his poems reflect the idealised romantic notions of war that many people held at that time.

Once described by Yeats as "the handsomest man in England". A view shared by just about everyone who met him, both male and female.

He lived at the Old Vicarage in Grantchester, there is a museum next to the old tea rooms. He is, ironically, buried in a foreign field.

The Hill

Breathless, we flung us on the windy hill,
  Laughed in the sun, and kissed the lovely grass.
  You said, "Through glory and ecstasy we pass;
Wind, sun, and earth remain, the birds sing still,
When we are old, are old. . . ." "And when we die
  All's over that is ours; and life burns on
Through other lovers, other lips," said I,
-- "Heart of my heart, our heaven is now, is won!"
"We are Earth's best, that learnt her lesson here.
  Life is our cry. We have kept the faith!" we said;
  "We shall go down with unreluctant tread
Rose-crowned into the darkness!" . . . Proud we were,
And laughed, that had such brave true things to say.
-- And then you suddenly cried, and turned away.

The Soldier

If I should die, think only this of me:
  That there's some corner of a foreign field
That is for ever England. There shall be
  In that rich earth a richer dust concealed;
A dust whom England bore, shaped, made aware,
  Gave, once, her flowers to love, her ways to roam,
A body of England's, breathing English air,
  Washed by the rivers, blest by suns of home.
And think, this heart, all evil shed away,
  A pulse in the eternal mind, no less
    Gives somewhere back the thoughts by England given;
Her sights and sounds; dreams happy as her day;
  And laughter, learnt of friends; and gentleness,
    In hearts at peace, under an English heaven.

Sonnet Reversed

Hand trembling towards hand; the amazing lights
Of heart and eye. They stood on supreme heights.

Ah, the delirious weeks of honeymoon!
Soon they returned, and, after strange adventures,
Settled at Balham by the end of June.
Their money was in Can. Pacs. B. Debentures,
And in Antofagastas. Still he went
Cityward daily; still she did abide
At home. And both were really quite content
With work and social pleasures. Then they died.
They left three children (besides George, who drank):
The eldest Jane, who married Mr Bell,
William, the head-clerk in the County Bank,
And Henry, a stock-broker, doing well.

The Old Vicarage, Grantchester

Just now the lilac is in bloom,
All before my little room;
And in my flower-beds, I think,
Smile the carnation and the pink;
And down the borders, well I know,
The poppy and the pansy blow . . .
Oh! there the chestnuts, summer through,
Beside the river make for you
A tunnel of green gloom, and sleep
Deeply above; and green and deep
The stream mysterious glides beneath,
Green as a dream and deep as death.
-- Oh, damn! I know it! and I know
How the May fields all golden show,

And when the day is young and sweet,
Gild gloriously the bare feet
That run to bathe...
`Du lieber Gott!'

Here am I, sweating, sick, and hot,
And there the shadowed waters fresh
Lean up to embrace the naked flesh.
Temperamentvoll German Jews
Drink beer around; - and there the dews
Are soft beneath a morn of gold.
Here tulips bloom as they are told;
Unkempt about those hedges blows
An English unofficial rose;
And there the unregulated sun
Slopes down to rest when day is done,
And wakes a vague unpunctual star,
A slippered Hesper; and there are
Meads towards Haslingfield and Coton
Where das Betreten's not verboten.

Εἴθε γενοίμην...would I were
In Grantchester, in Grantchester! -
Some, it may be, can get in touch
With Nature there, or Earth, or such.
And clever modern men have seen
A Faun a-peeping through the green,
And felt the Classics were not dead,
To glimpse a Naiad's reedy head,
Or hear the Goat-foot piping low:...
But these are things I do not know.
I only know that you may lie
Day long and watch the Cambridge sky,
And, flower-lulled in sleepy grass,
Hear the cool lapse of hours pass,

Until the centuries blend and blur
In Grantchester, in Grantchester...
Still in the dawnlit waters cool
His ghostly Lordship swims his pool,
And tries the strokes, essays the tricks,
Long learnt on Hellespont, or Styx.
Dan Chaucer hears his river still
Chatter beneath a phantom mill.
Tennyson notes, with studious eye,
How Cambridge waters hurry by . . .
And in that garden, black and white,
Creep whispers through the grass all night;
And spectral dance, before the dawn,
A hundred Vicars down the lawn;
Curates, long dust, will come and go
On lissom, clerical, printless toe;
And oft between the boughs is seen
The sly shade of a Rural Dean...
Till, at a shiver in the skies,
Vanishing with Satanic cries,
The prim ecclesiastic rout
Leaves but a startled sleeper-out,
Grey heavens, the first bird's drowsy calls,
The falling house that never falls.

God! I will pack, and take a train,
And get me to England once again!
For England's the one land, I know,
Where men with Splendid Hearts may go;
And Cambridgeshire, of all England,
The shire for Men who Understand;
And of that district I prefer
The lovely hamlet Grantchester.
For Cambridge people rarely smile,
Being urban, squat, and packed with guile;

And Royston men in the far South
Are black and fierce and strange of mouth;
At Over they fling oaths at one,
And worse than oaths at Trumpington,
And Ditton girls are mean and dirty,
And there's none in Harston under thirty,
And folks in Shelford and those parts
Have twisted lips and twisted hearts,
And Barton men make Cockney rhymes,
And Coton's full of nameless crimes,
And things are done you'd not believe
At Madingley on Christmas Eve.
Strong men have run for miles and miles,
When one from Cherry Hinton smiles;
Strong men have blanched, and shot their wives,
Rather than send them to St. Ives;
Strong men have cried like babes, bydam,
To hear what happened at Babraham.
But Grantchester! ah, Grantchester!
There's peace and holy quiet there,
Great clouds along pacific skies,
And men and women with straight eyes,
Lithe children lovelier than a dream,
A bosky wood, a slumbrous stream,
And little kindly winds that creep
Round twilight corners, half asleep.
In Grantchester their skins are white;
They bathe by day, they bathe by night;
The women there do all they ought;
The men observe the Rules of Thought.
They love the Good; they worship Truth;
They laugh uproariously in youth;

(And when they get to feeling old,
They up and shoot themselves, I'm told)...
Ah God! to see the branches stir
Across the moon at Grantchester!
To smell the thrilling-sweet and rotten
Unforgettable, unforgotten
River-smell, and hear the breeze
Sobbing in the little trees.
Say, do the elm-clumps greatly stand
Still guardians of that holy land?
The chestnuts shade, in reverend dream,
The yet unacademic stream?
Is dawn a secret shy and cold
Anadyomene, silver-gold?
And sunset still a golden sea
From Haslingfield to Madingley?
And after, ere the night is born,
Do hares come out about the corn?
Oh, is the water sweet and cool,
Gentle and brown, above the pool?
And laughs the immortal river still
Under the mill, under the mill?
Say, is there Beauty yet to find?
And Certainty? and Quiet kind?
Deep meadows yet, for to forget
The lies, and truths, and pain?...oh! yet
Stands the Church clock at ten to three?
And is there honey still for tea?

Xu Zhimo (1897-1931)

King's College

It seems appropriate to finish with 'Saying Goodbye to Cambridge Again' (A Farewell to Cambridge) probably written in 1928. Tragically Xu Zhimo died in a plane crash in China in 1931 at the age of 34. He still remains an important poet, especially amongst the young in China, hopefully for his poetry and not just his romantic life. His divorce created quite a scandal at the time.

There is a memorial, in the form of a stone of white Beijing marble containing the first and last two lines of this poem, at the back of King's next to a willow tree.

Saying Goodbye to Cambridge Again

Very quietly I take my leave
As quietly as I came here;
Quietly I wave goodbye
To the rosy clouds in the western sky.

The golden willows by the riverside
Are young brides in the setting sun;
Their reflections on the shimmering waves
Always linger in the depth of my heart.

The floating heart growing in the silt
Sways leisurely under the water;
In the gentle waves of Cambridge
I would be a water plant!

That pool under the shade of elm trees
Holds not water but the rainbow from the sky;
Shattered to pieces among the duckweeds
Is the sediment of a rainbow-like dream?

To seek a dream? Just to pole a boat upstream
To where the green grass is more verdant;
Or to have the boat fully loaded with starlight
And sing aloud in the splendour of starlight.

But I cannot sing aloud
Quietness is my farewell music
Even summer insects keep silence for me
Silent is Cambridge tonight!

Very quietly I take my leave
As quietly as I came here;
Gently I flick my sleeves
Not even a wisp of cloud will I bring away.